CW00552354

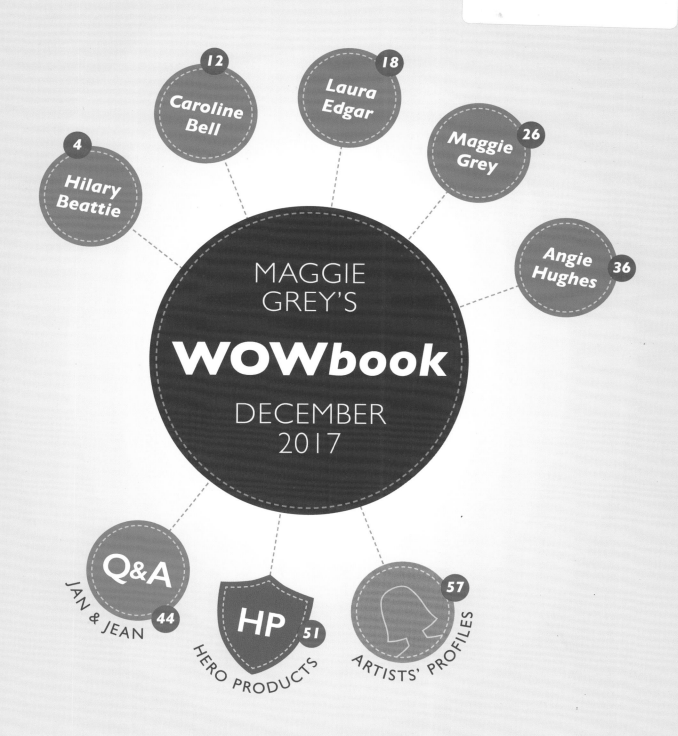

MAGGIE GREY'S

WOWbook

DECEMBER 2017

Welcome *to the first* WOWbook

Almost twenty years ago Clive and I started an online magazine which we called Workshop on the Web. The concept was simple – a quarterly online publication with great tutors writing step-by-step workshops, product and exhibition reviews and the odd bit of news.

We thought we might have a few hundred students but soon we had thousands and were quite overwhelmed. Luckily we found Fiona, who soon had the administration ticking over (she also found herself editing and writing articles but we never managed to convert her to stitch). WOW, as it became known, grew and grew and we were lucky then to find Sam and Amo to help us along. Facebook was a turning point, and having a private members' page was brilliant because at last we could see what people were making, and shots of their own work were inspiring for all of us.

So why buck the trend and make it into a book, when everyone else is going the other way? Well, partly, just because we could. Maggie was already a partner in d4daisy books and was finding a big overlap with Workshop on the Web. It also seemed to make economic sense as there is a high cost involved in running two businesses and taking payments online safely (and, with both companies, we always went for the highest security level). We did toy with the idea of a printed magazine but books are what we are used to and what we love. The WOW password system and website, once 'state of the art', were in need of a rethink so it just seemed to be the right time. If you have purchased the book, you will find that the new website has lots of great features and, because the passwords are contained within this book, we are no longer troubled by errant emails.

I hope you like the book and will make the most of all the offerings on the website. I am planning a course that will build up with subsequent books to a full exploration of textile art from design and sketchbook to stitched pieces.

Join us online (*www.wowbook.d4daisy.com*) and let us know what you think.

Maggie Grey

> Laura Edgar *Vintage Dome*

A local scene, a historic building on the seafront in Laura's home town of Whitley Bay, inspired this piece. The base is a vintage tray cloth with hand crocheted edges. Layers of sheer chiffons, fabrics and lace, some pre-painted with acrylic paint and tea stain, were collaged with hand stitching, including fly and long/short stitches, to create a nostalgic impression of the scene.

MAKE IT YOUR OWN
Design and stitch a unique hanging

Hilary Beattie

There are loads of beautiful commercial fabrics available to us these days – with which we can make some wonderful things. But there is nothing (in my view!) quite as exciting as starting off with white fabric and a great idea and then using simple skills to design and make your own materials. You can use these to make something unique and personal to hang on your wall – which is what we are going to do in this project.

I'll share techniques and ideas to get you going and producing, then provide some tips and guidance on how to use the gorgeous stuff you make. So with no more ado, let's get going … so exciting!

YOU WILL NEED:

- Cut Master hot stencil cutter (or similar)
- Glass paper (very fine-grade sandpaper)
- Mylar (or acetate)
- Setacolour Opaque fabric paint
- Procion dyes
- Plain white fabrics – cotton or cotton lawn is good
- Paper – I used layout paper
- Soda ash
- Paint trays and rollers
- Paper and pencils for design
- Wodge of paper or fabric to use as a drop-cloth

> Follow the steps in the article to make this lovely stencilled, dyed and stitched piece.

Designing the stencils

Start with a drawing or photograph of an image you like. Here I have used Echinaceas, one of my favourite flowers which I keep returning to in my designs. If it is a photo then look for easy-to-trace elements. Try to take photos fairly 'flat on' to make it easier for yourself.

I traced the drawing and simplified it, adding 'bridges' at the same time. A bridge is a small amount of the stencil material which is left between elements of the design to help it hold together. The easiest way to find out what works as a stencil is to look at some commercial stencils and then have a go. The worst that can happen is that it doesn't work and all falls apart. I have done this many times – and have learnt through this what works and what doesn't – and I still get it wrong sometimes. So what? I just have another go.

Having drawn up my main flower design, I made myself a design sheet with the main design facing both left and right (so useful when designing) and a couple of other all-over designs using elements of my drawing.

TIP

If your cutter seems to be cutting less efficiently, it may just be that it is clogged up. Take a sheet of glass paper and very gently sand the tip to get back to the metal

Making the stencils

It is possible to cut stencils with a knife but it is much easier with a hot stencil cutting tool. A soldering iron is too brutal, I find. I love my Cut Master stencil cutter. It burns through my Mylar (a plastic stencil sheet) at just the right rate for me.

So turn it on to heat up and then place your drawings under a clear glass sheet (mine is a worktop saver from Sainsbury's). Take the material you intend to use for your stencil (I find Mylar easier to burn than acetate) and place it over your drawing, on top of the glass sheet. Hold in place with small pieces of masking tape and then get ready to cut. The tool will be very hot after 5 minutes, so practise on a spare sheet of acetate while you get the hang of how it burns through the sheet. Then slowly and gently – you shouldn't need pressure – let the tool burn away around the lines of your design. When you are done, put the cutter down (I like to put mine in a ceramic pot to rest – seems safer to me) and lift the stencil. Poke out all the little bits and discard. If any don't come out, just be patient and recut them. Don't rip at them – you may rip your stencil (ask me how I know). And voila, a unique stencil.

Repeat with your other designs. You may need to sand the edges of the design gently, although I have found this less necessary as I have got more familiar with the cutter.

Admire your pile of stencils.

About paints and dyes

I use fabric paint on both fabrics and paper as it allows me to swap seamlessly between the two. I use Setacolour Opaque as the opacity is important when overdyeing (which we will be getting to later). There are other opaque fabric paints on the market but none as reliably and fully opaque as Setacolour.

With dyes I prefer Procion dyes, again on both fabric and paper. They work beautifully as an ink on paper and, of course, as a permanent dye on fabric. I mix the dye powder with water (about 1 teaspoon in 200–250ml) and keep that mixed up in jars in the studio. Use very hot water to dissolve the powder (and be sure not to inhale it – I wear a mask) and then top up with cold water. Procion needs a fixative, which is soda ash. If you add this to your dye mix, it becomes active, with a working life of about 4 hours. After that, it is inert and fabric will not be washable. To make it last longer pre-soak your fabric in a soda ash solution for about 15 minutes and then let it dry. Store this labelled as 'soda-soaked fabrics'. The dye in your pot will meet the soda in the fabric and become active. Neither the fabric nor the dye in pots goes off when kept apart. My dyed materials are very vibrant.

Note: you don't need the soda ash if you are working on paper.

Making materials – painting

Oh this is the bit I love best (I think). Get out some papers and fabrics (I use both interchangeably in my work), turn on some great music and have fun.

Choose a colour theme and put some paint out on your tray. I like to add a main colour (in this case, red), plus white and grey to make tints and tones as I work. I've also dolloped on some pink here to add some more variation to my materials. Roll out the paint in the tray with your sponge roller (much easier to use than either a brush or a brayer) and get stencilling.

Work randomly or in repeat patterns, whatever appeals to you. And try turning over the wet stencil, then with a dry brayer taking the paint off onto another piece of cloth or paper – you will get some lovely negative patterns. Keep tweaking your colour and adding variations with a little white and grey. It is also effective to add layers. I think layers of imagery are the big 'secret' of successful materials. Make some pieces with your all-over patterns and others with your main 'feature' stencils. Just have fun and don't stress.

Make loads. I made at least twenty times more than I needed but that just says 'work in series' to me – and I thoroughly enjoyed every minute. Plus – it is sooooo much easier to make a collage when you have a good selection of materials to choose from, rather than scrabbling and searching, so indulge yourself in a few hours of play.

TIP
Adding grey and white paint to the main colour adds variety and a bit of zing!

So now you have one pile of materials. Then mix up another tray with a different colour. I like to use a high contrast. In this case I've used blue and green, from the opposite sides of the colour wheel, but you choose a combination you like.

As before, add a little grey and white and get stencilling. Aim for a range of tones from light to dark. And try mixing your two paint palette colours on the same piece of material as well.

You should end up with a glorious selection of materials – all your very own.

Making materials – overdyeing

Get ready to be amazed. As long as you used a fully opaque paint, the overdyeing process seems like magic, creating the most exquisite, almost batik-like effect.

Get a nice wodge of paper or fabric to work on, which will soak up excess dye. I find a flipchart pad is excellent. Choose some dye colours you like, see page 5 for dye preparation, and find a nice fat mop-head paintbrush.

Then just slop it on, right over the paint.

Setacolour Opaque will resist the dye, so it just soaks into the gaps around the paint and looks stunning. You can overdye in any colours you like with opaque paint and get some fantastically exciting materials. Try different colours – even on the same piece. Just play and see what happens – there are no wrongs and rights … just differences.

Overdye some with lighter colours and some with darker. The more you do, the more addictive it gets. I overdyed the lot and ended up with loads of yumminess – makes me want to lick them all …

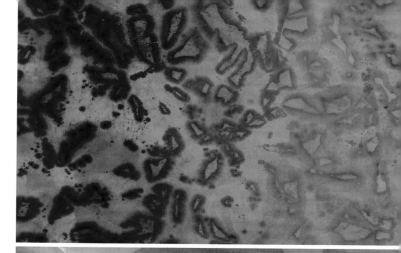

Design and make

Collage

So now you have an exciting pile of gorgeous, unique materials. You can either sit and just stroke them (you are not alone) or you can get straight into making some work with them (maybe after a quick stroking).

I love to collage down my materials onto a good-quality wool/viscose felt. I find this a very freeing way of working – and so easy.

First up, using one of your feature images, choose a size you would like to work to. I decided to work a 12in (30cm) square piece, which will fit onto a 12in (30cm) square canvas. You don't have to mount onto canvas but it does make such a nice finish.

So mark your dimensions on the felt. I'm using my canvas as a guide and a pencil to mark my square. Leaving about an inch (2.5cm) around the edge for straightening and trimming, extend your lines to the edges. This will allow you to see where the lines are when they are covered up with materials. You can see this in the pic below.

Now audition some feature images and choose one or two (I decided to make two collages alongside each other that can hang together). Don't forget to consider the backs too – sometimes they are more interesting than the fronts!

Having made your choice(s), start laying out materials on your felt and moving them around to see what you like.

There are no rules here – just go with what you like. The best advice I could give you would be to get the felt covered quickly. Just go for it fairly instinctively. Then – and only then – consider what you like, what you don't and why.

Here are some hints I share with my students:

- Starting is the hardest thing – so just do it – don't think. Put down three or four pieces anywhere and you are off! You can then start to make decisions about what to add and what to take away.
- What mood do you want? This will affect your choice of colour (fabrics) and your layout.
- Consider your focal point. Is it where you had planned? Or has a different one sneaked in? Moving away from the piece, or using a digital camera, can help you to get a good perspective.
- Then decide if you need to enhance your focal point to draw the viewer's eye and add impact. Colour and line are useful elements to consider here.
- What sort of movement (or not) have you got in your collage? Does it fit with what you wanted? Is the viewer's eye being directed around your piece as you would wish? Colour, contrast, line and shape are helpful here.

Most important, enjoy the process. Let yourself have as much or as little time as it takes. Sometimes I can get a collage working in just 10 minutes. Other times it can take days or even weeks. It will be the same for you. And remember – the only opinion that matters is your own.

Once you are happy, take a photo for reference and then back all the pieces with Heat'n'Bond (or Bondaweb if you prefer). Replace the piece, adhesive-side down (no need to trim) and, using a hot iron, stick onto the felt.

Stitching

This collage turned out to be all paper – but that is fine because paper stitches very nicely.

Set your machine up for free machine work with a darning foot and feed dogs down. On my machine, I find I can usually stitch through all the layers well with an 80/12 quilting needle. However, if you find threads breaking or stitches skipping then maybe try a 90/14.

Also make sure you have a strong thread. I prefer cotton and so use mostly Superior Threads King Tut as it is so strong and reliable. Pick colours that blend with the areas of your collage and get threaded up. I like to use Superior Bottom Line in the bobbin. It is very fine but strong and I just have white, pale grey, mid grey and black. I find this better than matching top threads in the bobbin, but do whatever works for you.

Then settle down and enjoy some nice stitching. Start by outlining the feature flowers so you know where you are and then fill in the background with whatever patterns you enjoy stitching. I've used a lot of circles as they seem to mimic the bubbliness of the Echinacea heads, and then some 'wonky lines' to fill in the rest of the background.

Once the background is filled, go back into the feature flowers and machine embroider them to pull them out from the background. How much you do is your choice – I like to go over edges and add petal details for emphasis.

So now you have a beautiful stitched collage and there is no reason at all why you couldn't just leave it at that. But I do like to take the opportunity to tweak colours and contrasts using a combination of artists' pencils, crayons and gelatos. I love using these anyway and it is another chance for a colouring session.

For example, I had embroidered a leaf from the original paper when quilting and extended it into the green area. So I can now use my pencils to add colour to the parts that are just outlines.

I also used a pencil of the same colour to bring up the Echinacea flower and then added some contrast with a white pencil – all helping make this the focus of the piece.

So the whole image is now coloured – looks better I think.

Still wanting more contrast for my feature flower, I used a white Neocolour 1 crayon to lighten the background around the flower. And finally a pinky gelato to just soften the deep red/pink edge a little.

Sometimes I do a lot more tweaking than this but I felt that was enough here. I then sealed with ultra-matte acrylic wax for protection and, after doing the same for the other collage, I have a lovely pair.

These can now be finished any way you choose. I like to trim them and mount on canvas using Pebeo matt medium to stick them down. I used some more of the materials to 'bind' off the edge of the piece and around the canvas, which gives such a nice clean finish.

Stick them up on your wall – and admire!

immunity from beauty

^ This textile, which used an echinacea plant as
a design source, was printed on layout paper.
Using simple but effective techniques, it was
then overdyed and stitched before being
mounted over a stretcher.

A NATURAL CONCLUSION
Eco-printed paper tiles

Caroline Bell

There is a great deal of interest in textiles at the moment and we are all so much more aware of the damage we can do to our environment. That's why, some years ago, I became interested in using natural substances on natural fibres such as silk, wool, linen, cotton and paper.

Although at first my interest was more to do with an awareness of the harmful effects of some of our textile processes, I was also thrilled with the effects that I could achieve.

YOU WILL NEED:

- 5 or 6 sheets of A4 paper. I used abaca tissue which has great wet strength. The process works with most kinds of paper but if you wish to stitch into your tile afterwards, it is better to use a finer paper such as thin khadi paper or even thin wallpaper lining paper which seems to print very well
- A pair of ceramic tiles. Mine are the 20 × 25cm (8 × 10in) size, obtainable from any DIY store, often quite cheaply
- 4 large (5cm/2in) bulldog clips, the kind that fold over on themselves
- An old paintbrush
- Some iron water. I used a ferrous sulphate solution, 1 teaspoon to a litre of water, but you can make your own with old nails or wire wool left in a jar with half vinegar/half water for a couple of weeks. If you would rather not use iron water then you can substitute with plain water. However, the prints may not be quite as dark
- A large pot, big enough to take your tiles comfortably. Please note that this will not be suitable for the kitchen after you have used it for eco-printing. I bought my pots variously at car boot sales, auctions, Asian food shops and charity shops
- Leaves. I have used a variety of Japanese maples. Other leaves good for printing include oak, sycamore, blackberry, geranium and dogwood. Note that not all leaves print but, while some flowers give good prints sometimes, they do not give reliable results all the time. This summer I have been experimenting with Coreopsis flowers and these have been most successful
- Cotton muslin: a fat quarter or 50 × 50cm (20 × 20in)
- A piece of polythene a few centimetres bigger than the muslin
- PVA glue
- Some neutral-coloured thread

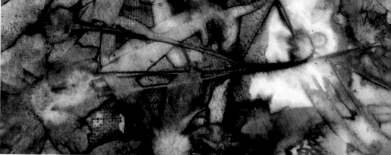

Method

Stage 1

Fold your paper in half, place it on one of the tiles and open it out. Then paint the iron solution all over. Arrange the leaves over one half and fold the other half over the top so that you have a leaf sandwich. Repeat with the other pieces of paper so that you have a stack of sandwiches on your tile. Then place the other tile on top of this. Take the bulldog clips and place one on each side of the tile, thereby firmly clamping the leaf sandwiches inside.

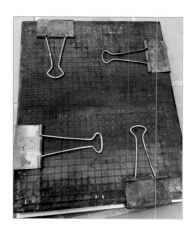

Flip the clips over as in the pic left, which will help the tiles fit into the pot. If you cannot source these particular clips, you can tie-up the tiles firmly with string but this may not give the same kind of pressure, which is the secret of clear prints.

∧ These paper tiles show the results of this method of eco-dyeing. They have been enhanced with simple stitching.

Bring a pan of water to the boil and simmer gently for about half an hour.

Note: it is better to overestimate rather than underestimate your timings.

To avoid burnt fingers, it is better to take the package out of the pot and allow it to cool a bit. Then, very carefully, open the package and take the leaves out of each individual sandwich. You will probably need to do this quite quickly as the leaves tend to stick to the paper if it is allowed to dry out too much. Do not worry if you get a few rips or holes as you are going to tear up the paper at the next stage in any case. Allow the paper to dry.

Stage 2

Hopefully you are now in possession of some nicely printed sheets of paper. You now need to tear them up into about 5–6cm (about 2in) random-size pieces, making sure that some of these include whole leaf prints. At this point you should select the very best prints and set them aside in a pile, putting all the other pieces with indifferent prints, or no prints at all, in another pile. Dilute your PVA by 50% with water. Place your muslin on the piece of polythene and liberally cover with the PVA. Using the pile of indifferent or no prints, begin to paste onto the muslin until it is covered.

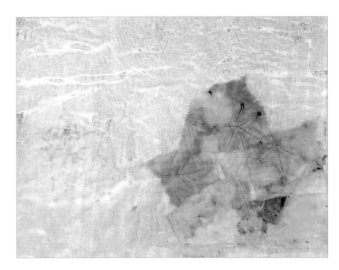

Then, using your better prints, add a second layer. Make sure that all the muslin has a good coverage of paper and that it is all well stuck down. Leave to dry – depending on the time of year this may take a while, possibly even overnight.

Stage 3

You should now have a dry piece of work backed onto muslin. At this stage you can optionally give it a covering of beeswax (painted on and ironed off) or acrylic wax to give it a bit of stability, but this is not essential. Using a 15cm (6in) tile (or make a template), select an area which appeals and, using the template, draw round it and cut it out. I managed to get three out of my fat quarter piece. I also cut out some more shapes to layer up on my tile. To soften the sharp-cut edges, carefully introduce them to a flame (preferably a candle), being very careful not to set your piece on fire – keep a bowl of water nearby, just to be on the safe side.

Stage 4

Your pieces are now ready to be stitched. This is the bit where you can personalise your work and make it your own. It can be as simple or as complex as you wish. Alternatively, feel free to follow what I have done in the pics right or, at least, use them as a starting point. Because of the rigidity of the surface, negating the need for a hoop, it is an extremely pleasurable process. Happy stitching!

> These stitched tiles
> demonstrate the
> harmonious range of
> colours that can be
> achieved using Caroline's
> eco-printing techniques.
> The simple hand
> stitching is the perfect
> foil for the rich patterns.

NORTHUMBERLAND SUNSET
Applied fragments on fabric

Laura Edgar

This inspirational photo was taken on my mobile phone during a family day out in my local region. I was inspired by the atmospheric sky and the focus is on the dramatic light and movement in the sunset and clouds. With some pieces, I may do some sketchbook work or refer to my mood boards on Pinterest. Along with this visual imagery, as with all my work, I then begin to gather and collect materials which may be suitable for the artwork.

I always start by looking through my fabric hoard, which consists of recycled and vintage clothing and textiles, gathering small snippets and larger pieces in the colours of the image. At this point I am also thinking of what it is about the image that I would like to convey to the viewer, looking at the colours, textures and movement and thinking of possible techniques that may be used. I am also thinking about whether it will be a piece worked onto a fabric base or a piece straight onto an artist's canvas; these are the two main ways in which I work.

My work incorporates pre-painted or dyed textile fragments and I enjoy experimenting with painting or mark-making on various fabrics, as well as other methods of manipulation such as heat.

For this piece, I used acrylic paints mixed with water or tea to paint the sky and clouds onto a piece of silk slightly bigger than the finished piece. I placed the silk on some thin white sketchbook paper or newspaper, then wet the silk with tea and painted the sky in acrylic onto the silk. The paper will stick to the back of the painted silk in places and this can give some interesting sculptural effects when dry.

I scrunched the silk and creases appeared where the paper adhered to the back, giving some aspects of the movement of the clouds.

I use regular artists' acrylic paints, the main colours of my palette for this piece being Payne's grey, ochre, prussian blue, white and mars black. I mixed them with tea in the water, which dulls the colours to the natural, subtle hues that I am after. They were then applied to the silk in varying thicknesses; wetting the silk first with the tea or water so that the paint spread or bled to create interesting watermarks. I am after spontaneous results.

∧ *Northumberland Sunset.* Collage techniques can be
applied to fabric, using a variety of materials. This work
perfectly captures the atmosphere of the photograph, while
enhancing the textural elements.

Marking out the piece to scale on the background

The background cotton or linen was measured out, allowing a little space either side for a wider range of framing or mounting options. With a water-removable pen, a rough sketch, including the horizon line, was marked on the background fabric of the main basic composition.

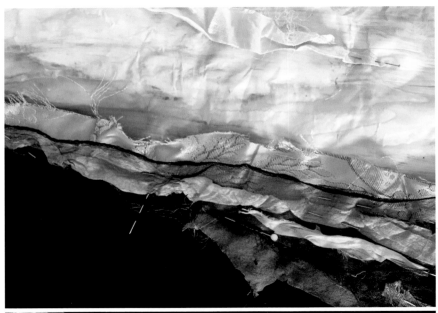

Collage

I then gathered together the painted silk sky along with my other collected fragments and began to compose the base and to create the basic composition of the artwork. For this piece, I started by placing down the painted sky after choosing to keep it whole, as some interesting marks, which could be enhanced, had emerged. I added a large dark piece of fabric for the bottom half of the composition (from a jersey knitted top) and a strong yellow fabric for the horizon (curtain fabric). This was followed by some irregularly cut pieces of silk and sari scraps to highlight the reflection on the water. These pieces were pinned and tacked down and acted as the base on which many layers of fabric and stitch would be worked. The stitches were tone-on-tone, basic irregular running stitch worked in a sketchy manner, and they were not removed; they became part of the work, adding to the texture.

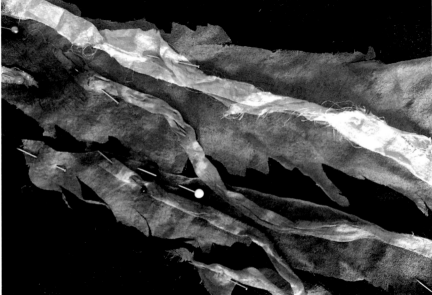

Horizon

For the horizon, I maintained the intensity of colour by layering fabrics of different tone: sheer black chiffon over the yellow, densely woven patterned curtain fabric which had a sheen that is dulled in parts by the dark chiffon, creating contrasts of light and shade. I manipulate fabrics by hand and like to work with their natural properties; different fabrics have different effects in the way they fray, crease or fold – hence I tend to store my fabrics scrunched up in a box rather than flat! I also do not flatten them on the work itself, stitching them down only so that they don't move and using threads of various thicknesses in sketchy running stitch to highlight areas.

Sky

To emulate the movement and textures of the clouds, I began by building up layers of soft, sheer fabrics such as silk and chiffon, cutting them roughly into the shapes of clouds, fraying them, allowing spontaneous irregular shapes to be created, then pinning and stitching them into place. To highlight the various densities and textures of the clouds, I used fragments of crochet doilies and also sari scraps with subtle dyed colours. These were stitched with various thicknesses of threads, regular sewing cotton and embroidery threads using freehand running stitch and fly stitch with tails to create texture and movement.

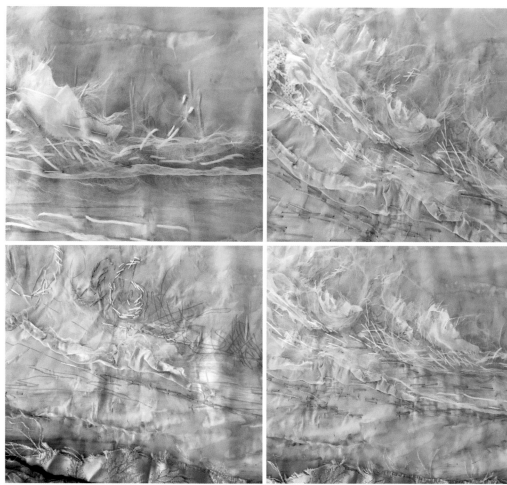

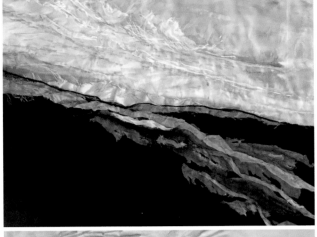

I tend to assess the piece at certain points of its creation and I find that looking at it from a distance, a different perspective helps assess which areas need more work.

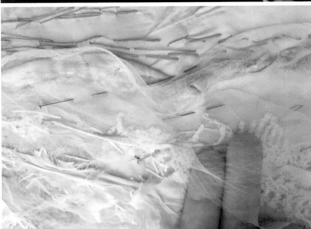

Having looked at the sky, I saw that I needed to build up the texture and movement of the clouds. Adding more layers of chiffon and hand-stitched details in various thicknesses of thread created colour variations and shading.

Sea

The base of the sea is a dark background with some silk and sari fragments cut into irregular organic shapes to replicate the light on the water, with black chiffon overlaid. To create the movement of the water and the light of the sun reflecting on it, I created my own lace using soluble fabric. There are many water-soluble fabrics on the market; I like to use the opaque variety rather than the clear, plastic type. I marked out the pattern that I wanted to create with a water-removable pen and checked its position on the fabric.

You can see the pattern, below left.

This design was then stitched on the sewing machine using running stitch and overlaying with zigzag stitch. The pattern needed to interweave like a web. When held under running tepid water, the fabric dissolved, leaving a lace-like fabric ready to be placed onto the base.

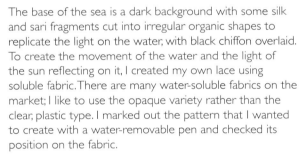

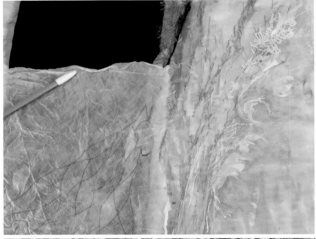

Manipulated chiffon was overlaid on the bottom
part of lace to create depth, shading and contrast.

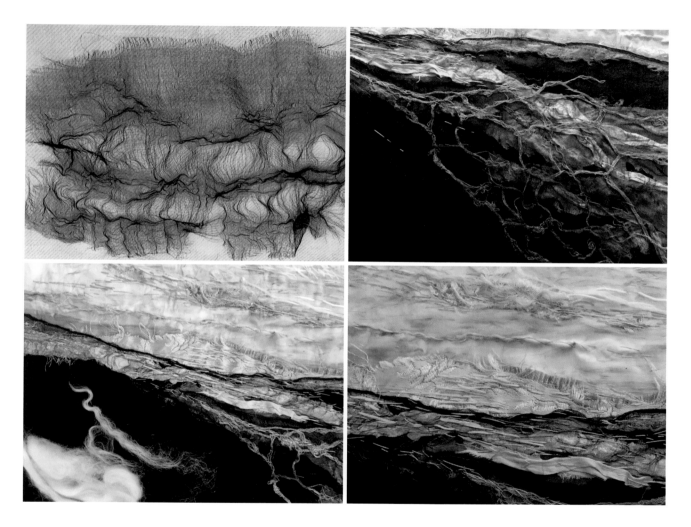

At this stage, the piece was assessed again to decide where
more colour or stitch was needed. The colour of the sun in the
sky below the clouds needed to be more intense, so I layered on
more yellow fabric and layers of bold yellow stitching. To soften
some of the sky and create areas of light and shade, I added grey
and white merino wool and also yellow, raw, curly sheep fleece
to blend areas. These were stitched down with visible stitching.

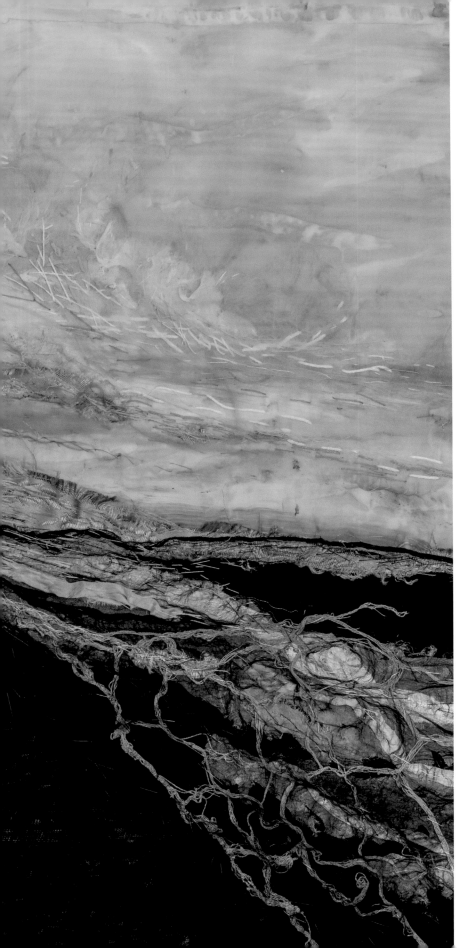

I do hope this description has inspired you to look not only for inspiration but also for ways of using colours, textures and movement in your work. Don't forget to take a good look around the charity shops and vintage stores.

Australia

If you feel inspired by this workshop, here is another piece, see right, worked in the same way but depicting the glorious skies in southern Australia, experienced during my 2016 tutoring trip. This is the demo piece for one of my residential workshops, which was worked from a photograph. Layers of pre-painted and bleached papers were collaged with further layers of vintage lace and recycled fabrics to depict a sunrise over the sea. Free, spontaneous hand stitching in running, long/short and fly stitches, in threads of varying thickness, was used to create movement and texture. Lace, made using water-soluble fabric on the sewing machine, formed a further layer on the sea, and merino fleece on the sky helped to create further shading and texture. The horizon was free machine stitched to pull it back and recess into the horizon in the distance. I wanted the viewer to be drawn into the image, to feel the atmosphere.

< This detail of *Northumberland Sunset* shows the effect of the water-soluble fabric and of the zigzag and running stitch.

RIVER CHAT
A narrative vessel

Maggie Grey

This is really two articles in one. In the first part I describe making a three-dimensional vessel. However, at a stage in the making process I laid out the pieces in a box frame and was struck by the fact that they looked good as a piece of mounted work. So I made both.

The idea for a piece of work based on a song had been in my head for a while, and the round *River Chat* by John Warner is a favourite with the acapella group I belong to.

The song was featured in a Protest in Harmony, Wateraid rally and I was delighted to learn that John Warner is an Aussie (plenty of water issues in Australia) so I had lots of material in the form of sketchbooks to draw from (I've taught over there many times). I had some good email chats with John when I asked him for permission to use his lyrics.

River, river where do you flow
with your water the colour of tea,
Golden red in your sandy bed,
do you flow to the wide, green sea?

No, said the river, I flow inland,
Sink down deep among the rocks and the sand,
Under the gidgee and the mulga tree,
Where the desert people can drink me.

Earth belongs to all, she belongs to no one,
she belongs to herself.
Earth belongs to all, she belongs to no one,
she belongs to herself.

As a starting point, I looked out my sketchbooks and travel diaries from trips to Australia. The lyrics of the first verse suggested to me the rivers in the Northern Territory which, in some parts, have a reddish tinge from the soil. We had been shown wonderful rock paintings of the Ang-bang-bang people and I'd reproduced a lot of these in my sketches. I did make sure that none of the places was a sacred site as I think you have to take care not to ride roughshod over other people's beliefs. Our guide assured me that these could be viewed as early selfies, so all was well.

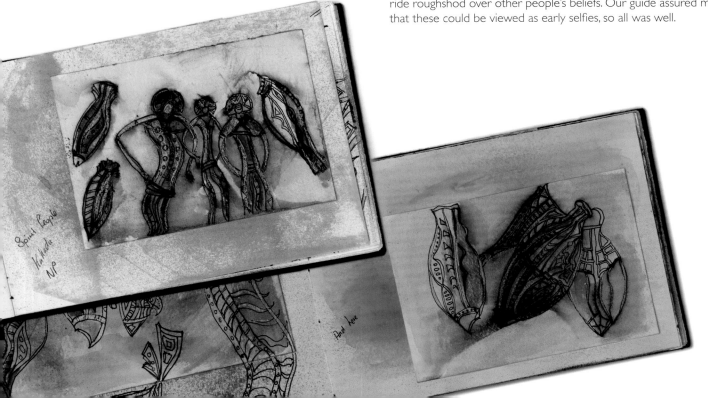

> This vessel was used as a vehicle to convey the lyrics of a song about the precious resource of water, particularly in Australia. Sketchbook drawings were traced onto tissue paper before being bonded and stitched to form the sides. They were then stiffened with Wireform and the 'river' was formed with wrapped pipe cleaners carrying 'tabs' of text.

I had been experimenting with ways of laminating paper, fusing painted tissue on top of crumpled printer paper, and thought this would work well, with images traced from my sketchbook on the tissue and printed maps on the heavier paper. So that was the decorative element sorted.

∧ Tissue paper drawings were prepared and laminated onto computer prints of maps of the region.

Making the vessel

I always like a three-sided vessel and mine don't have bottoms (I suppose technically they are not vessels at all). As the song is about a river, there obviously had to be water somewhere, so that was a consideration.

My initial plan was for a large vessel but I thought it wise to make a small one first to ensure that the idea and the structure hung together well. In fact, due to a light-bulb moment part way through the making, it turned into a river in a box as well. Read on.

Laminating the papers

I also searched out some online maps of the area. As I enjoy stitching into paper, the maps seemed a good idea for a background and I printed them out and crumpled them up until the paper was soft and stitchable. A favourite technique of mine is a form of laminating paper – bonding the surfaces together.

Painted tissue paper on top of printed paper always works well and allows a glimpse of the lower sheet through the upper. It is also quite strong when bonded and takes stitching well. Drawings from the sketchbook were traced onto the painted paper to produce the pieces shown here.

Here is how it is made

1. Cut a piece of Tissuetex paper the same size as the printed map (mine was A4). Then lay it on non-stick baking paper and wet it with a brush and some water. This is done so that the paint colour in the next step is not too strong and will show the print below it – in this case it will be the map.

2. Use a liquid paint – it could be Brusho, Adirondack spray, Koh-I-Noor, watercolour, or anything similar. I used a teabag and a dash of yellow, brown and orange watercolour paints. The better brands of paints give a clear, strong colour which is good for laminating papers.

3. While the Tissutex dries, trace off (or draw) some motifs from the sketchbooks (or design source) onto cartridge paper, copying a variety of figures and fish – or whatever your inspiration. Isolated shapes are best as you can then make tracings from them and put them together in a variety of ways. Trace the motifs onto the painted tissue with a pencil.

4. Enhance the tracings with watercolour pencils, using a dark one for the edges and adding a little more colour where needed. Instead of activating the watercolours with a brush, try gently touching a wet-wipe to the paper. Use a white watercolour pencil to add a few little highlights. Mine mimicked the original white pigments in the paintings.

5. When all is dry, crumple the tissue well, very carefully so as not to tear it, and bond it on top of the crumpled map. I prefer the lighter bonding webs for this, so try something like FuseFX or Misty fuse. Be careful not to press too hard when ironing or you will flatten the papers too much. Check that it is stuck – and then leave it to cool.

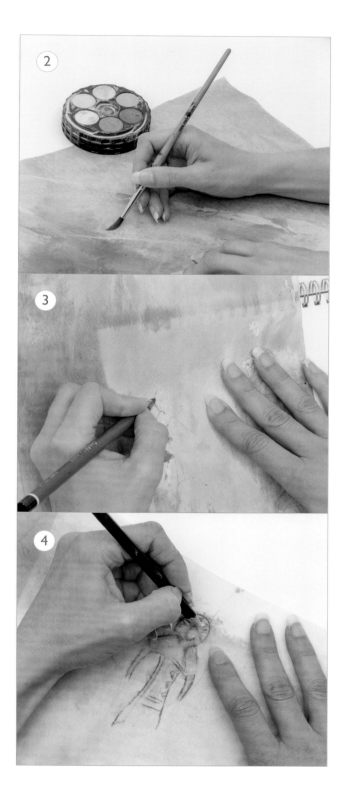

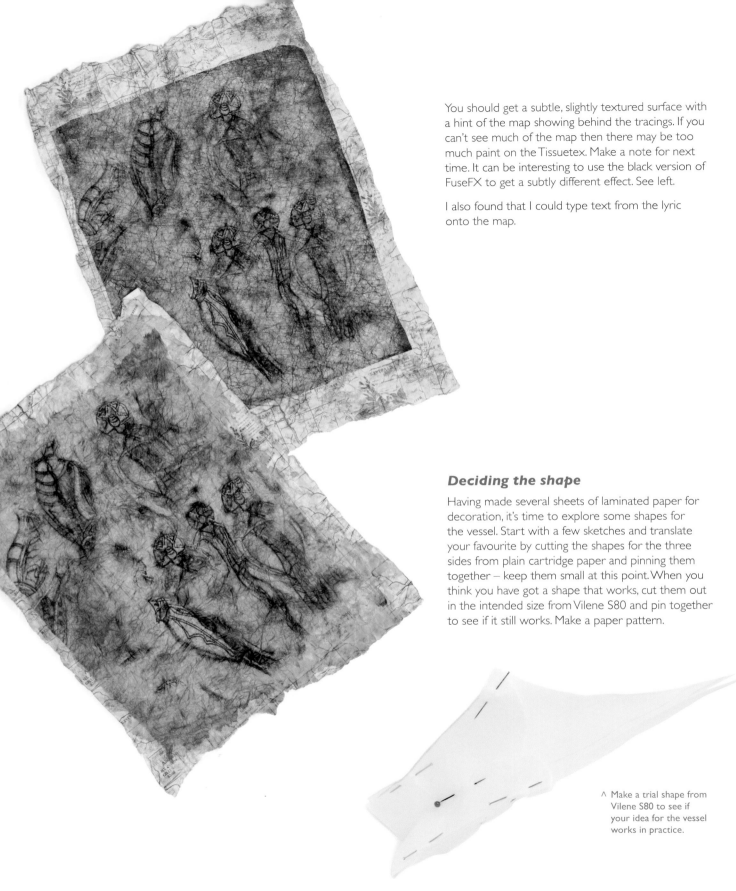

You should get a subtle, slightly textured surface with a hint of the map showing behind the tracings. If you can't see much of the map then there may be too much paint on the Tissuetex. Make a note for next time. It can be interesting to use the black version of FuseFX to get a subtly different effect. See left.

I also found that I could type text from the lyric onto the map.

Deciding the shape

Having made several sheets of laminated paper for decoration, it's time to explore some shapes for the vessel. Start with a few sketches and translate your favourite by cutting the shapes for the three sides from plain cartridge paper and pinning them together – keep them small at this point. When you think you have got a shape that works, cut them out in the intended size from Vilene S80 and pin together to see if it still works. Make a paper pattern.

∧ Make a trial shape from Vilene S80 to see if your idea for the vessel works in practice.

< In this pic (left to right) you can see: tea-stained Vilene for lining, Wireform, unpainted Vilene for stabilising the top and finally, the laminated paper, cut to size.

Your shapes may be entirely different, so it is important to try several options and then make a pattern. The use of Wireform – a bendy type of metal mesh – gives the option of adding a curved shape to the structure – elements can be bent into waves and wiggles. It also adds strength. It does mean that you use more Vilene, as it is essential to trap the scratchy Wireform safely between two layers of Vilene.

When happy with the Vilene shapes, cut an extra piece for each side from Vilene and dab with tea or paint with pale colours. This will form the lining.

Then, *very carefully,* cut a single shape for each side from Wireform. Cut this very slightly smaller than the Vilene pieces so the edges are enclosed. I use stout gloves when cutting it and would suggest binding the edges with masking tape. Cut the laminated paper to fit on top of the unpainted Vilene. Layer them up to make sure they are all the right way round as it is easy to get muddled.

In the pic above (left to right) you can see: tea-stained Vilene for lining, Wireform, unpainted Vilene for stabilising the top and, finally, the laminated paper, cut to size. The lining is shown right side up but it will turn over to fit (wrong sides together) when the sandwich is made.

Stitching

Now it's time to stitch the laminated paper to the unpainted Vilene. If the cutting is correct, it should fit exactly on top. I cut two of the pointed pieces and a bridging piece, shown here, to join them together. In the pic right, the laminated paper partly stitched to the Vilene is shown together with the lining.

As the vessel will not be washed, you can use a very small amount of adhesive such as Golden acrylic medium, to stick the laminated paper to the Vilene shape, but take care not to make it too stiff as it will be stitched. As ever, there are now choices to be made about the stitching, depending on whether you like to hand or machine stitch. In either case, as the 'fabric' is quite busy, stick to simple stitching.

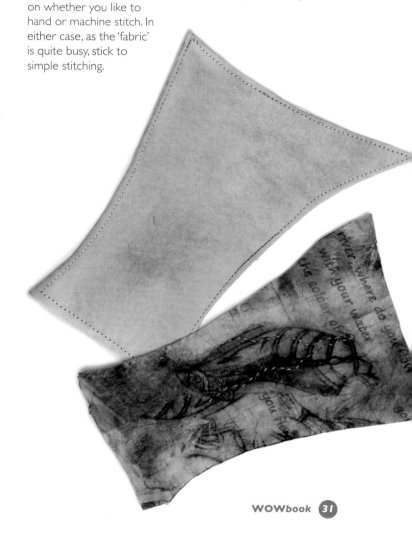

Hand stitching

Work simple hand stitches into the tissue/Vilene sandwich. It's too fussy to stitch around each shape so I simply worked wavy lines of running stitch over the top. Any simple surface stitches such as chain or feather stitch would be good. The random wavy lines gave me an idea for borders which will be shown later. Trim the edges, if necessary.

Machine stitching

Simple lines of machine stitching served to fix the tissue firmly to the Vilene. These were completed with the foot on and feed dogs up, as for normal stitching.

Joining the pieces

When the laminated paper is securely stitched to the Vilene, it is time to join it to the lining pieces, trapping the Wireform inside the sandwich. This will form the sides of the vessel.

Go back to the cut-out Vilene — both the stitched piece and the lining — and place them all together, trapping the Wireform between the stitched Vilene and the tea-painted lining Vilene. Stitch, using straight stitch, all around three edges, as close to them as you can get. Do not stitch the top edge — I find hand stitching gives a better finish here.

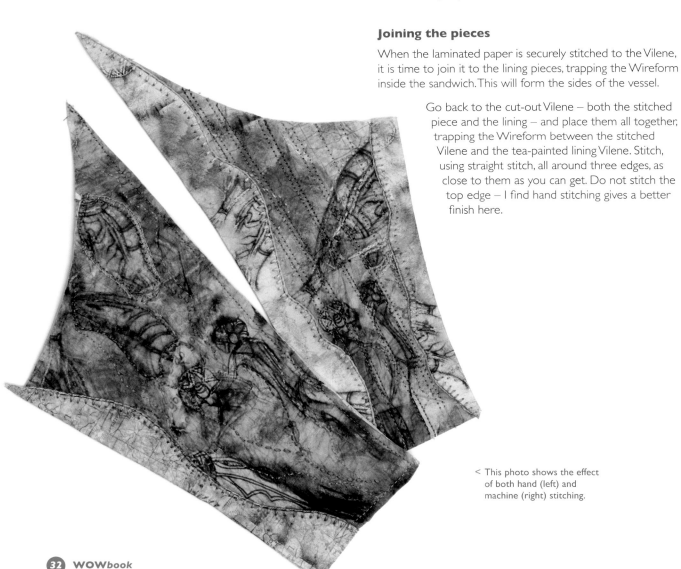

< This photo shows the effect of both hand (left) and machine (right) stitching.

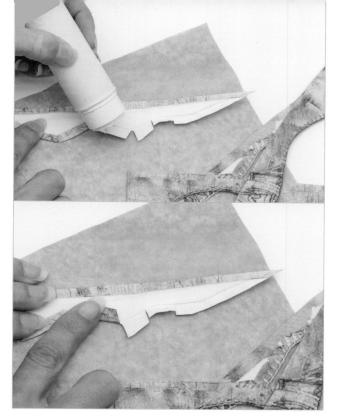

Constructing the vessel

Wiggly borders

Borders can enhance and unify the segments. I have laid these over the pieces in the photo to check the effect but they won't be fixed in place at this stage. This pic also shows the different effects of hand and machine stitching.

To make the borders, either paint paper (ordinary printer-weight paper is best) or scan your laminated paper and print it out. Crumple it up to make it soft and then use off-cuts of Vilene, cut into shapes to fit the edges they will cover, adding gentle curves. Cut the shape from the paper, leaving an overlap to fold to the back. Apply Golden medium to the front of the Vilene and press the paper on firmly. Turn it over and snip the excess paper to fit around curves before gluing that down firmly. Add stitching – I used buttonhole – if you wish.

Joining the seams

Here are two ways to join the edges – I sometimes use both on one vessel, as I have here.

METHOD 1

Just place the wrong sides together and oversew with a narrow satin stitch all along the seam. As you can see, I have left the top open as the Wireform allows interesting movement. The top has been buttonholed.

METHOD 2

Join the seam, right sides together, and cover with one of the edging strips. The seam is effectively hidden. Stab stitch to join.

I often leave a point at the top of the border strip. This can protrude or be cut level with the edge.

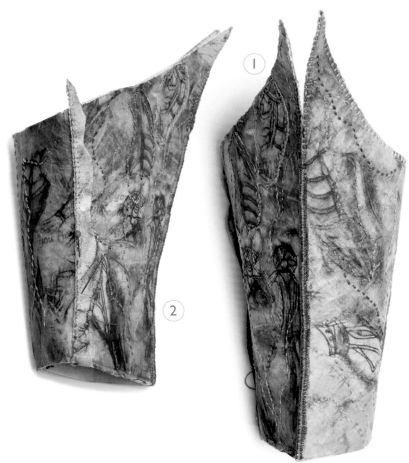

Finishing the vessel

Now is the time to neaten the top and lower edges with buttonhole stitches, which will pull all the layers together. Machined satin stitch will work as well, but can look a bit heavy.

Before you join the final seam, stop and look at the shape of the piece you have made. If it looks good, go ahead and join the final seam. This will have to be a 'wrong sides together' join as it would be difficult to turn the rigid shape inside out. I decided to leave one seam open to give a view into the interior of the piece – partial deconstruction. The top couple of inches (5cm) of the long seam was also left open so the points could be turned outwards.

Almost there now, just a few final steps:
- Give the exterior of the vessel a coat or two of acrylic wax. It will protect the tissue surfaces and give just the hint of a gleam.
- Add any exterior decoration such as small tassels from the points, or braids with attached beads or small drilled shells.
- Contour the sides, bending them gently into shape, held by the Wireform. I just made a gentle curve.

The river

It seemed to me that my 'river' could be made of wrapped pipe-cleaners, bent into wave shapes, cascading down the interior of the vessel.

< Detail of wrapped pipe-cleaners and text tabs.

Fancy yarns were wrapped around the pipe-cleaners and some small beads were stitched onto them. Beads shaped like bones (bound to be a few of those with all those crocodiles about) were also added. I fastened all these together at the top to resemble a waterfall.

Further braids were constructed using the sewing machine, as described by Angie on page 38. I loved her idea for making a cord on dissolvable fabric. Where she made leaves, I made some little fishes. I made sure that Angie was happy for me to use her idea (such a good one) in this way.

Finally, the waterfall was threaded through the points of the vessel and pulled down to nestle between them.

Having thought that it was finished, I walked away and left it for a few days, returning later for another look. I find this helps me decide whether a piece is finished, as I am a great one for overworking. Taking photos of the 'possibly finished' work is good for this as well.

My only concern was that the lyrics had not come over as well as I had hoped, so I made three 'tabs' to hide in the river of wrapped pipe-cleaners. These tabs were made from small rectangles of tea-dyed Vilene S80, with torn printed paper pasted on top. This seemed to do the trick.

Deconstructed vessel in box frame

You may remember that I had earlier threatened to take my vessel to pieces as it looked rather good in a box frame. So I made some more shapes in just the same way, placing them in a box frame over tea-dyed watercolour paper overlaid with some lettering stamped on fine Lutradur. The river was made by painting Pebeo Prisme paints on metal shim and letting it dry really well. Set between the borders, it produced just the result I'd hoped for.

VANISHING WORLDS
Collage and layering techniques

^ Angie has used a variety of techniques for this piece, including transfer paint, machine embroidery and zapped chiffon.

Angie Hughes

I'm always inspired by gardens, hedgerows, trees and leaves. This project comes from my imagination; half-remembered images of vetch tendrils, ivy creeping up a rough tree trunk, the black buds of an alder in my garden and a dark ferny corner under a quince tree.

You will be making components, then collaging them all together at the end.

MATERIALS AND EQUIPMENT

You will be working with earth tones, greens, some zingy limes and oranges, so choose your colours with this in mind. The project is small, so pieces of felt and film need be no bigger than A4.

- Transfer foil
- Sheer fabric organza
- Kunin felt, yellow or green
- Firm iron-on Vilene
- Bondaweb fusible webbing
- Transfer dyes: suggested colours are bright blue, golden yellow, magenta
- Water-soluble fabric
- Iron and ironing pad (needs to be a hot iron) and baking paper
- Soldering iron
- Table cover
- Photocopy paper, 6 sheets
- Paintbrush, sponges etc.
- Plate, jamjar
- Variegated embroidery machine threads
- 2 metres of piping cord or crochet cotton for wrapping
- Sharp scissors
- Sewing machine with foot suitable for free machine embroidery
- 8in (20cm) wooden embroidery ring
- Basic sewing kit: scissors, pins, needles, hand-stitching thread

Transfer printing

You will need some pots of disperse dye to get started. In this project we will use golden yellow, bright blue and magenta. Mix a solution of 20g in 500ml of water. It will last quite a while in a bottle, so you don't need to use it all up at once.

Paint the solution onto some printer paper – 100gsm is a good weight, not too absorbent. You need the dye molecules to 'sit' on the paper ready to be transferred. Paint two or three sheets of plain colour, then you can mix the liquid colour on the paper experimentally, just to see what happens later.

Set up an iron and board. The board could be a piece of wood covered with cotton wadding and a bit of calico. Nice and flat. Place a piece of kunin or eco-felt on the board: I find that starting with a coloured felt works well. Your iron needs to be very hot. A heat press would be great but I like the random prints you get using an iron.

Place your painted paper face down onto the felt and iron. Move slowly. Don't leave the iron in one place too long or you will get a transfer pattern of the iron's soleplate.

Lift away the paper to see if the colour has transferred. If nothing much has happened, turn up the iron temperature and try again. If after two or three attempts nothing has happened, I'm afraid to say it's probably your iron; you'll need one with a bit more wallop. Some travel irons are surprisingly hot.

Try putting some resists down. Hand-cut paper shapes work nicely, or pop into the garden and pick a few leaves.

The way to get interesting results is to keep changing the papers – some of the plain colours and some of the mixed colour ones – so that the colour changes with each print. It's a sort of blending technique. Try different leaves and different background colours.

Cord wrapping

There are lots of ways to wrap cords and wire to add into your collage. Set the machine to zigzag and free machine embroidery. Drop the feed dogs.

In this project, you can use any cord. In this case, I've used a crochet cotton – quite a thin one. Variegated threads are great for cord wrapping; you can get a nice 'natural' look. Zigzag over the cord quite quickly, moving gently back and forth while holding the cord under tension. Move along the cord, covering it with thread. If you hesitate in places, you will get a build-up of thread that looks quite knobbly, which is another way to give your cord a natural look.

Using water-soluble film

Another way to make interesting vines and tendrils is by using water-soluble film. I use a heavyweight one, folded in two. First, stitch a continuous line with free machine embroidery up and down the film, leaving a space between to stitch little leaves onto the cord. Then go over the line with zigzag to give the cord a bit of strength and substance. Now go over it again, stitching the little leaves, attaching them with further stitching as you go.

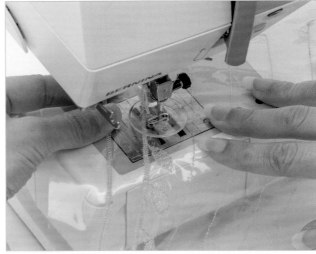

The easiest way to stitch a leaf is to start stitching with a simple outline then scribble back and forth over the leaf shape, going slightly over the outline shape. Remember that everything needs to connect. Otherwise, when you wash away the film, you will end up with a bundle of disconnected thread.

I also made another cord like this but, instead of leaves, I zigzagged on the spot every now and then, building up the thread to make a knobble.

Wash away the film by soaking in water for about half an hour. Then leave it to dry.

Take the cord that you wrapped at the beginning and the knobbly cord you made with water-soluble film and zigzag them together with the same coloured variegated thread you used for the original. I have used a very limey green thread for the knobbly cord, so they really contrast well.

The knobbly cord also works well when intertwined with the leafy one.

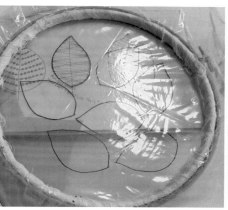 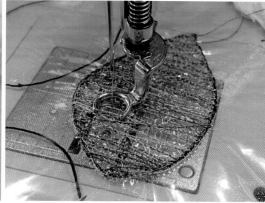 

Making leaves

Lay a piece of organza underneath a piece of water-soluble film. Cut pieces big enough to go into an 8in (20cm) embroidery hoop. I've been studying simple leaf shapes that are easy to stitch, so tracing them from my sketchbook onto the film is an easy way to transfer designs onto fine fabrics without making a mark on the fabric. Free machine embroider the leaves any way you like. My stitching is very simple as I want them to appear fragile.

When you've finished, cut out the leaves and soak the film away. Leave them to dry. They curl up a bit, which gives a great three-dimensional look to the piece.

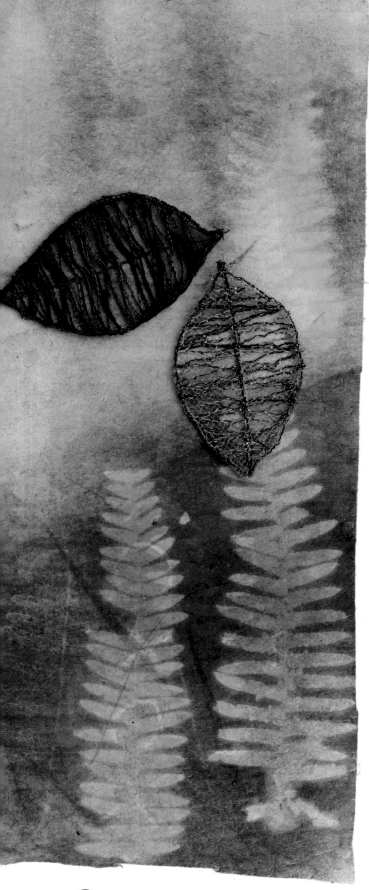

A bit of twinkle

The last component in this project is some rough texture. This was inspired by the chiffon sandwich in Maggie Grey's book *Raising the Surface*. My interpretation uses organza, the same colour as the leaves. You will need two pieces of organza, two pieces of Bondaweb and some gold transfer foil roughly A4 size.

Place some baking paper, a little bit bigger than the organza, on your ironing board. Place one piece of organza down and iron the Bondaweb onto it.

Peel away the Bondaweb paper. Foil the Bondaweb with a cool iron by placing the foil onto the Bondaweb, colour side up.

Cover with another piece of baking paper and iron firmly with one stroke. Peel away the film from the foiled surface. Place the second piece of organza on top and repeat the process.

Peel the sandwich off the parchment as it will have stuck. Then lay it back down and pin the four corners to the ironing board. Using a hot air tool, zap the sandwich until it has lovely golden crusty holes all over.

You can rip this piece up and add it to your final collage.

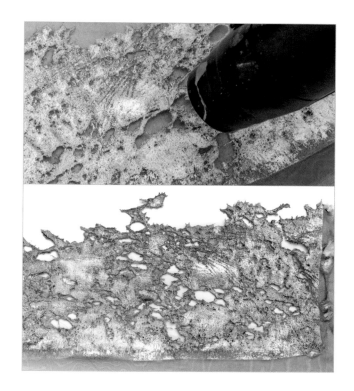

Tying it all together

Take your favourite piece of transfer printed kunin felt and apply a piece of firm iron-on Vilene to the back. This will help to stabilise the felt for free machine stitching. You can do as much or as little free machine stitching as you like at this stage. I've just outlined my fern a little bit with the lime green thread I've been using.

Rip up the organza sandwich and place it onto the felt. I've got a bit of a formula for the arrangement, so this textured piece takes up about a third of the surface and is usually placed on the right-hand side. Stitch over this texture with wiggly free stitching in a complementary colour thread. You could stitch some spirals to make them look like knots in a tree trunk. I changed the top thread to a 12 weight, a thickish topstitch thread. I also use a 16 topstitch needle for this. Changing thread colour and weight adds interest to your machine embroidery.

>The 'chiffon sandwich' has been applied to the transfer painted background to add texture.

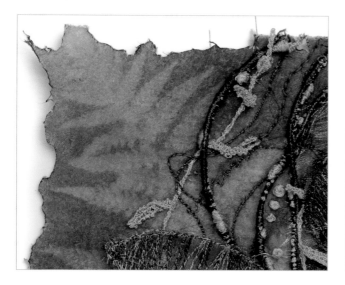

Now you can have fun arranging your cords and leaves on the surface. Play around entwining them, poking the leaves in and out until you have something you like. Take a photo of it so you can remember the placement.

You can now stitch on your cords and tendrils by hand if you like. If using the machine, I usually hop around, zigzagging on the spot here and there until everything is held in place. Then snip out the connecting threads between each zigzag. I don't stitch everything down perfectly. This gives you options to poke a leaf behind a cord later if you feel it needs it.

Now you can stitch on the leaves and, this time, I've done it by hand using just a couple of small stitches, here and there. To finish off, you could add some hand stitches. My favourites are french knots and seed stitch. Maybe a bit of beading too.

My final decision was whether or not to take a soldering iron to the edges. As the felt reacts well to heat I did, but if you try this, be careful to observe health and safety considerations. Work on a heatproof surface and keep a jar or mug handy on which to rest the soldering iron. Mind your fingers.

< The leaves and cords are arranged on the surface of the work.

There are lots of variations on this technique and you can see more ideas on the WOWbook website

DOUBLE TROUBLE, DOUBLE JOY
Jan Beaney and Jean Littlejohn talk to Samantha Packer

Q The hugely popular exhibition *25 Years Then and Now* was held at Knitting & Stitching Shows in 2016 and celebrated your partnership, key pieces of your work and the books you have published together. How did you approach the curating and selection of material for an exhibition based on such a large body of work?

A The new work was an important element for both of us and although we were each aware of the general nature of the other's work, we really didn't know how they would look together until we put it up at the show. Somehow it seemed to work.

We wanted the overall look to have simplicity and the samples we chose very much reflected comments we had received over many years of teaching classes. We framed them quite simply in white frames to make the show less cluttered. We were careful to ensure we had at least one example from every book. Some of our sample pieces were resolved and suitable in scale to stand as finished work and the selection of the work was quite organic. Some pieces almost selected themselves.

∧ *Moongate* (approx 18 × 18in, 46 × 46cm). Jean Littlejohn.

< Pavement sketchbook. Jean Littlejohn.

> Small pavement pieces. The series was entitled *Full Circle* and these are six of twelve, each based on a month of the year (approx. 5 × 5in, 12 × 12cm). Jean Littlejohn.

Q Your collaborations as Double Trouble, publishing books and DVDs, show you working independently on a shared theme or product. Have you always felt it important to work individually rather than collaborate directly on pieces of work?

A People are often surprised that we live close to each other but do not work together. Our styles are very different but our philosophy is similar. We both need to be really engaged with the subject and work through themes, sometimes over many years. Thinking about and researching the work and producing technical samples are important parts of our practice.

JEAN: Following through from our last exhibition, I have been continuing along the notion of time and the natural calendar. Important seasonal markers such as the solstices, equinoxes and cusps continue to fascinate. I also include elements related to our ancestors throughout history. We are part of a continuum and I hope to include some essence of history and the passing of time in my work.

< *Harvest Moon* (approx 18 × 18in, 46 × 46cm). Jean Littlejohn.

∧ *Cliveden: Winter Vista.* Appliqué, hand and machine stitching on Solufix before being backed with scrims. The embellishing machine was used to unify and blend in some areas (24 × 48in, 61 × 122cm). Jan Beaney.

JAN: I always work in themes – Crete, Australia, and my local field have been favourites. I did make six panels based on my garden, four of which were colour drifts, trying to capture an essence of the plants without being too literal. These, together with the pond series, were also shown in the *25 Years Then and Now* exhibition I am now ready to embark on another theme based on Cliveden House and Estate, a location belonging to the National Trust that has fascinated me for years. I made a body of work inspired by the location from 1975 to 1978 but since then I have continued to look more closely, to draw and experience new vistas, unexpected and fleeting light changes on a range of subjects and surfaces. The formal aspects and the wilder elements of the estate present a challenge on how best to combine them into unified designs that capture the essence of the place. So it is a case of 'watch this space'!

This year has also seen the production of our new DVD, which is over five hours long and split into chapters. It is called *Interpretations – Look – Record – Draw*. We hope to de-mystify the many drawing and colouring materials that are available and to demonstrate a variety of approaches and techniques. We believe that everyone can learn to draw, certainly enough for them to collect useful information to inform their work in order to make it personal and unique to them.

It is important to work individually on our own pieces. When collaborating on a book or DVD, we do have brief initial discussions and a rough outline structure but, on every project, we have worked independently for much of the time, quite deliberately so that our audience does get two separate views, albeit with a shared philosophy. We also do not want to over-influence each other. It helps that we really understand each other's strengths and that is there in the background. We have never duplicated and are always amazed when we come together nearer the time at just how it all fits together.

∧ Sketchbook page: *Greek Island of Lesbos*. Study and collage of prickly shrub (approx. 6 x 16in, 15 x 40cm). Jan Beaney.

> Sketchbook page: *Australia, Trees at Uluru*. Jan Beaney.

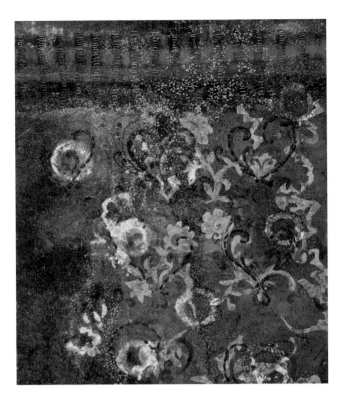

∧ *Reclamation: Victoriana*
(approx. 29 × 18in, 75 × 45cm).
Jean Littlejohn.

∧ Sample: *Japanese Anemone.* Tap paper print onto Solufleece with
machine embroidery (approx. 7 × 9 in, 18 × 22cm).
Jan Beaney.

Q You are currently working on a new exhibition.
What can you tell us about it?

A We were thrilled to be invited to exhibit in Florida from
19 January to 10 February 2018. The exhibition is called
Textile Meditations: Mary Fisher and Friends and is to be
held at the Armory Art Center, West Palm Beach,
Florida, USA.

We have known Mary for many years, having initially met
her on our courses before working with her in her studio.
She has always been a great supporter in every way.

Q You became Joint Presidents of the Embroiderers' Guild
in 2012. How do you feel that the organisation has
responded to the changing landscape of textiles and
embroidery in the past five years?

A We are very anxious to support and promote an
organisation that has been a very important element for
many years. There have been tough times and necessary
changes but now we are in our new partnership at the
Buckinghamshire County Museum at Aylesbury. The
Embroiderers' Guild Collection – an independent and
significant body of pieces – is at last in a location with
museum status and controlled specialist conditions, which
is a marvellous move. By appointment, members will
be able to visit and study at the museum. This was an
important factor in making the decision to move there.
We now have a permanent home and there are many
exciting plans in the pipeline. So the future is looking good.

> *Long Garden: Spring*
(19in, 48cm square).
Jan Beaney.

Q How do you balance your work as textile artists with the responsibilities of promoting the Embroiderers' Guild?

A There is no conflict between our voluntary work on behalf of the Guild and our professional practice. The Guild structure has changed and made considerable advances to satisfy changing issues related to charities, health and safety issues, and safeguarding that are required by law.

We also have a new board of trustees, each of whom has committed to carry out a task that may concern IT skills, marketing, education, finance or any part of a standard business practice. They are working very hard and effecting changes in the light of altering circumstances. They are tremendous and, among them, we have a fantastic artistic director, Anthea Godfrey, who works tirelessly to promote the Guild. We are in a great position to move forward. Terry Murphy (CEO) and many volunteers did a magnificent job of organising the move of the offices and the collection from Kings Road to Aylesbury.

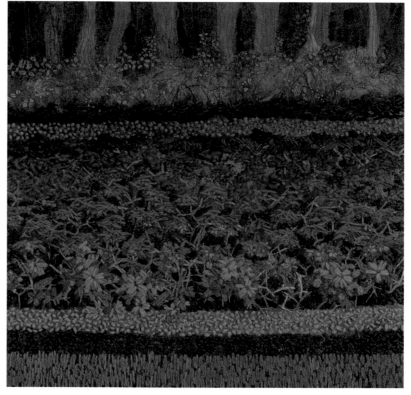

> *Long Garden: Summer*
(19in, 48cm square).
Jan Beaney.

∧ *High Cliff*
(approx 24 × 24in, 61 × 61cm).
Julia Caprara.

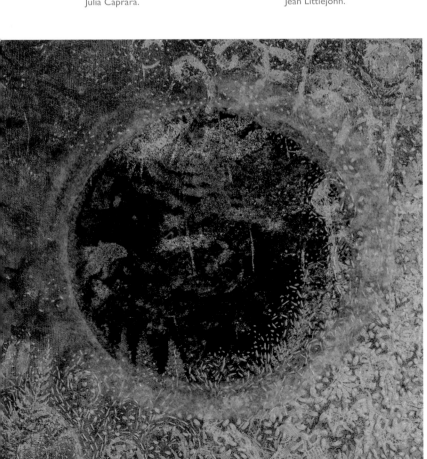

∨ *Snow Moon* detail
(approx 18 × 18in, 46 × 46cm).
Jean Littlejohn.

Q Next year will be the tenth anniversary of the sad loss of Julia Caprara. She was a powerhouse in the embroidery and textiles world through Opus School of Textile Arts with her husband Alex, forming Prism among many other things. As a good friend of hers, what can you tell us about Julia, her work and the impact she had on the world of embroidery?

A It is hard to believe that it is nearly ten years since Julia died. She was a dynamic woman with amazing energy and committed to encouraging students and professionals through the organisations she initiated. Her tutorial skills are evidenced in many exhibitions where we see her former students and their success. People who knew her cannot have been untouched by her vision and philosophies.

It was a privilege to curate a retrospective exhibition at the Knitting & Stitching Show. The many visitors were able to see just how much integrity and passion there was in this extraordinary woman. We miss her as a colleague but mostly as our lovely friend.

Q There are so many choices now in the materials available for use in both mixed media and textile art. What would you choose as your 'Hero' products?

JEAN: I would have to say the embellishing machine was a game changer for me. Solufix and Solufleece have also been important.

JAN: I have used and promoted soluble film/ materials, Solufix/Aquabond (sticky soluble), since the 1980s. The sticky one is the most useful. Collectively, we agree that we both love chenille no.14 needles and Koh-I-Noor water-based dyes which have featured regularly in the creation of our work over the years.

HERO PRODUCTS
Soluble solutions – so many options

BY: Amanda House

Following a hasty consultation with Maggie, I have been busily asking all and sundry about their favourite product. A surprising number have declared that they love water-soluble but find the various films and fabrics confusing. Yes, they can have you in quite a spin but, if you look a little more deeply, there really isn't too much to confuse and plenty of scope to play.

< Bowls made using Romeo film, shaped while wet.

∧ This scarf was made by covering the end of a strip of fabric in film and working from the fabric onto the film to create a lovely edging effect.

Most soluble fabrics are a seaweed-based alginate 'plastic' or web that, when wetted, will disappear. This is one less thing to worry about if you don't like to put things down your kitchen sink. It is also safe to empty the water onto the compost heap if you prefer.

Basically, there are two main types of the film, one a heavyweight and the other lightweight. There are also dissolvables that look like fabric and, just to confuse further, they come in a sticky version where one side has a paper backing, covering the glue.

Some of the names you will hear are Romeo (heavy), Soluheavy (heavy), Giulietta (light), Avalon (light) and Aquabond or Solufix (sticky). The fabric type, Solufleece, looks like dryer sheet or interfacing and it is sometimes easy to muddle them but you just have to wet a corner to check you have the right thing. Just to add to the choice, there are also films that are dissolved with boiling water or heat from an iron but I think we will stay with the cold water-soluble film, the fabric and the sticky. These should just about cover most of your needs. A fourth product is soluble paper which is, literally, just that. It looks a little like fine blotting paper and it doesn't take much for it to turn into a mush.

Film

The heavy film does not need to be hooped to work on the sewing machine. It is stiff enough to take a fair amount of thread, which can be useful. However, if you know your stitching will be really heavy, you can hoop it as with any fabric to reduce buckling. It is quite difficult to mark before stitching so it's best for free-form work. You can also use it if you want to link together two items of fabric or embroidery by placing them on top, perhaps lightly tacking them down with a bit of water-soluble glue stick, and stitching across the space to add a lacy link.

Solufix

This was the winner in the 'best loved of all' category, perhaps because it is so versatile. This sticky fabric is wonderful for keeping inclusions and threads exactly where you want them to be. If you place the fabric on your desk or a board non-sticky-side down, you can lightly tape down the corners as you remove the paper backing to have some control over it. Always keep the backing sheet to hand to cover the sticky, or everything you don't want will find its way onto it, including the cat! If you have a pattern or drawing you want to follow, you can slip it under the sticky fabric, making sure you have a good free margin all around. You can now follow the lines by placing threads and yarns on the sticky fabric. Areas can also be filled with snippets of fabric or chopped-up thread.

∧ Toffee papers linked by dissolvable film. The lightweight film should be hooped before use. You can always double it in the hoop for a bit more strength but any more than that and you are better off using the heavyweight film. Again, this is a difficult film to pre-mark.

> Maggie Grey made a sample for a waistcoat using Solufix with crochet motifs, chains and wool fibres placed on the sticky side. The piece was then free machine stitched before being dissolved. Having decided that the sample worked well, she has now drawn the full-size pattern on the dissolvable material and it is currently a work in progress.

When you have placed everything down to your liking, cover with a piece of lightweight soluble film and, starting from the centre, press it into the sticky surface as best you can. There will often be just a few spaces left and, hopefully, plenty around the edges to secure. This stops the foot of the machine becoming snagged on anything you have laid down. It also prevents it sticking. You can now un-tape it from your desk or board and take it to the sewing machine. When stitching, be sure to link all the areas or it will fall apart when dissolved. If you were following a pattern, as described earlier, it is easier to see where to stitch with see-through film on top. Then you can be sure that the lines and the filled areas are correctly stitched.

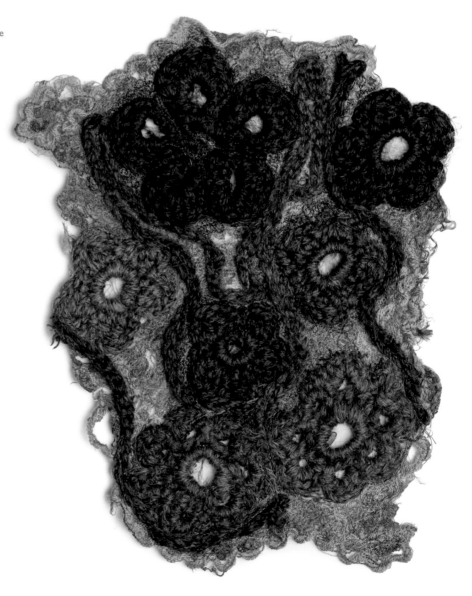

˄ Glynda Morrison placed wool tops
and a variety of yarns and fibres
onto the sticky side of Solufix. These
were covered with a piece of net to
strengthen them. She used vermicelli
stitch to hold the 'sandwich'
together before rinsing off in warm
water. The fibres formed a solid base
from which to cut pattern pieces.
Glynda found just the right piece
of coloured felt to complete the
making of this lovely garment.

Solufleece

Solufleece fabric has a soft feel and is white in colour. You can easily mark this using water-soluble pencil or crayons. It's best to use a pencil of a similar colour to your stitching, especially if using lighter threads. I love making a whole new fabric by sandwiching snippets of fabric or threads and yarns between two layers of Solufleece, carefully pinning and then stitching in linking swirls all over, being careful of the pins and removing them as you go. Depending on the density of your sandwich filling and stitching, you can achieve either a solid new fabric or something quite lacy after the Solufleece has been dissolved.

When using any of the soluble fabrics your stitching must interlink! The best way of ensuring you won't see your hard work floating off is first to stitch a grid, either regular or more organic and wavy, to make sure that at least the underneath is linked to start with. Make sure one, preferably two or more, lines of stitching touch and overlap other lines of stitching or inclusions. If you want to add hand stitching or beads, it is best to do this before dissolving the soluble fleece as it makes it far easier to handle.

< Snippets of yarn pinned between layers of Solufleece, stitched and dissolved. The resulting fabric was used to make a garment for the *White Figure*.

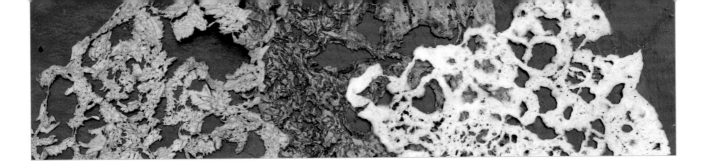

^ Left to right: water-soluble paper showing the effect of different strengths of tea. Some of the samples have been ironed when dry.

Dissolving

When you have finished, you then have to ensure that it has been stitched sufficiently well to stay in shape (or will be re-shapeable) Otherwise it will need extra stability by pinning out.

Loosely stitched pieces and some intricate borders will become just a heap of threads when they are dissolved. The easiest way to treat them is to pin them out on a piece of polystyrene packaging or tile, making sure you catch all the awkward stitched shapes with a pin, before running under the tap; or leaving on an upside-down bowl with a weight on it.

^ This pic shows a lacelike structure dissolved on a polystyrene tile.

Although all these materials are classed as cold-water dissolvables, I find that having the water slightly warm works better. Either run under a tap or use a bowl, changing the water regularly. You can also leave the piece in the water for an hour or so – overnight is even better. This will make sure the last of the gum is dissolved. When you are happy that all the sticky has gone, or there is still a little left if you want your piece to hold a shape, take it out of the water and place on some greaseproof or silicon paper to dry. Do not put it on paper towels or it will stick, no matter how well you have rinsed it.

Dissolvable paper

Dissolvable paper has several uses for the mixed media artist. It can be torn into smallish pieces and placed over a mould, a stamp or something with interesting texture. It can then be wetted with a paintbrush, which will turn it into a translucent porridge. Push it around with a brush or your finger to make sure that it fills all the crevices of the shape. When left to dry, it will reform into a paper, this time in the shape of the object into which you have pushed it. If you have made the paper thick enough, it will also take stitch beautifully.

For something that cannot be stitched, or just needs blending into a background, wetting and pushing the paper around the edges will create a stitchable edge that will hold the more solid object and/or blend it into the background quite nicely.

You can machine stitch into the paper directly but, as you would with all the other solubles, you must make sure the stitches are all interlinked before dissolving. A fairly tight scribble is quite effective but the paper will perforate and fall away if the stitching is too close.

If you very briefly dunk the stitched piece into water and quickly lift it out onto a Teflon sheet, the paper will pull up against the stitches with a little encouragement from brush or finger. This creates a lovely aged and worn look.

If you want the paper to be coloured, the best and easiest way to achieve this is to use strong tea, dirty water or watered-down paint as your dissolving water to start with. As you can imagine, using wet paint on a dissolving paper could be a disaster unless you are very careful with minimal paint on a very dry brush! You must also remember to seal the surface with acrylic paint or one of the Golden mediums.

This is just a brief look at dissolvable films, fabrics and paper. There are many ways of using them to make your own bases and fabrics as well as additions to other work. If you want a more in-depth look, try Maggie Grey's book *Dissolvable Delights* (published by d4daisy books). Many of Jan Beaney and Jean Littlejohn's books also have great ideas for dissolvable fabric.

ARTISTS' PROFILES
Who's who in this book

Hilary Beattie

Hilary is an artist who likes to design and make her own materials with fabric, paper and paint and then use these, together with commercial materials, to produce quilts and collages that reflect the beauty she sees in the world around her.

Hilary says, 'My passions are colour, form and imagery. At the moment, my main interest lies in expressing the wonder I feel when looking at the many beautiful things in our world. I expect this will change many times during my life – there again, maybe not. I want to share my experience of these elements which are both vivid and graphic. I see a beautiful world, despite its ugly aspects, and this drives me to depict this vision. It is life affirming, healing and important.'

She feels she is lucky to have friends who share this passion and, together, they intend to change the world. Believing that we are all artists, lacking only in the confidence to utilise this gift, she has recently started making some more personal work, based on her experience of living with depression, which she hopes to put together as an exhibition at some point.

Hilary started showing her work three years ago and, in that time, she has won many awards and now exhibits widely both as a solo artist and as a member of several groups. Showing her work is of great importance to her and has resulted in sales both in the UK and overseas. She has also recently published her first book in what she hopes will be a long-running series, looking at ways into design.

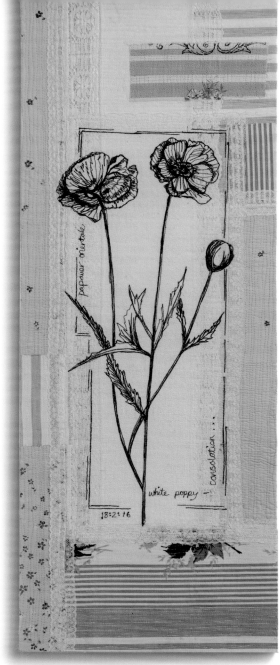

∧ In Victorian times, each flower had a hidden meaning, so posies could be made to convey a message for the recipient to 'read'. Based on this idea, Hilary made a 'posy' of works on canvas to give hope to those in despair. As a sufferer from depression, Hilary felt that this was especially relevant. The opium poppy stands for the relief that oblivion can bring as part of medical treatment.

< *Favourite Things*. The design for this quilt was inspired by Hilary's love of the vibrant Echinacea. A mix of commercial and her own printed, dyed and stamped fabrics were collaged onto a cotton ground and free machine quilted. Painted fabrics were applied for the flowers and leaves.

Caroline Bell

Caroline has worked as a textile artist for a number of years and, during that time, she became concerned about practices in the textile industry that had a negative impact on the environment. She decided to transform her own practice and began to research natural processes and more ethical ways of working. This she did within the framework of further study through a degree in Stitched Textiles.

On graduation, she was awarded an Embroiderers' Guild Scholarship which she used to develop a body of work based on the dye and print potential of materials gathered from her local urban green space. There was a lot of interest in the results of her research and the variety of colours and effects that she was able to achieve. She has exhibited widely in the UK and mainland Europe, both as an individual and as part of two exhibiting groups, Room 6 and Zero 9 textiles. In addition to producing her own work, Caroline regularly gives talks to a variety of groups and delivers workshops in eco-printing, natural dyeing and screenprinting with natural dyes.

Working on natural fibres – silk, wool, linen, cotton and paper – she colours and marks with natural substances by a process which involves applying heat and moisture to plant materials. This results in a print, derived from the chemicals within the plant transferring itself to the material. The effect is endlessly unpredictable and surprising due to a myriad of variables – the outcome of the process ensures that no result is ever duplicated. Caroline combines this technique with the use of natural dyestuffs, many of them harvested from her own garden or various places in her own locality.

Caroline loves fabrics that have had previous lives: old table linens or the off-cuts from the bed linen industry. She is often to be found scouring charity shops, car boot sales and antique shops for such treasures, and not only for these but for the tools of her trade – old pots, utensils and tools – which are all useful in many of the techniques she utilises She finds the process of creating something beautiful out of sometimes unpromising materials extremely satisfying.

A process-driven artist, enjoying the journey as much as the destination, Caroline devotes considerable time to dyeing, printing and growing raw materials. During the quiet winter months, she stitches almost exclusively by hand and makes work from the fruits of these labours. It is not surprising therefore that nature, time and the passing of the seasons are recurrent themes in her finished work.

∧ These wonderful scarves show the exquisite detail of Caroline's work.
∨ A pure silk is used as a base fabric and this has a delicate pattern in the weave which adds to the effect.

Laura Edgar

A textile artist and tutor based in Whitley Bay, northeast England, Laura works in textiles and mixed media, exploring a mix of vintage textiles, recycled clothing, paint, haberdashery and hand and machine embroidery to create original textile artworks, prints, handcrafted fashion accessories and cards. Fascinated by art from an early age, she discovered textiles as a medium of self-expression at school and from knitting, sewing and crocheting with her grandmothers. As a child, Laura would attend jumble sales with her mother and she still owns a few treasured pieces, including a pair of intricately hand-crocheted gloves. To this day she is a collector of vintage things, and a beachcomber.

A Foundation Studies diploma course gave her the chance to experiment before specialising in Textiles at Nottingham Trent University. After graduating in 1996, she worked for many years as a freelance textile designer, creating embellished embroidered fabrics for the fashion market. She also worked for a commercial embroidery designer, while creating textile artworks for sale at art and craft fairs. She now combines her artistic practice with being a mother and a civil servant. She has concentrated on establishing herself as a professional textile artist and tutor, exploring textiles as an art medium. Her work is sold in galleries across the UK and she teaches nationally and internationally; in 2016 she was invited to tutor in Australia.

Laura is inspired by the dramatic land and seascapes of her local region. She loves the ephemeral changes to light and colour that occur with the play of elements on our sea and landscapes. She is also inspired by the work of impressionistic painters, such as Vincent van Gogh, as well as Mark Rothko and JMW Turner. In the textile art world, the work of Geta Bretascu, Kaffe Fassett, Cas Holmes, Josefina Concha and Ana Teresa Barboza inspires her.

The sculptural qualities of textiles as a medium excite Laura. Changing the textures by the manipulation of paint, heat and embroidery techniques pleases her. This experimental approach is an important part of her work, which alternates between full textile works and mixed media pieces. She also likes the challenge of working straight onto a pre-stretched artist's canvas, using glue and a lot of papers, manipulating the glue and fabric in a sculptural way before layering with paint and stitch.

Initial inspiration is recorded with photography, sketchbook drawings and collage. Suitable textile fragments are gathered and the manipulation processes begins. A spontaneous, experimental approach allows the finished piece, which can be semi-abstract or representational in form, to develop. Laura is passionate about promoting textiles as an art medium, pushing its boundaries and its ranking within the art world, blurring the line between craft and art. To her, as an artist, textiles is her chosen mode of self-expression.

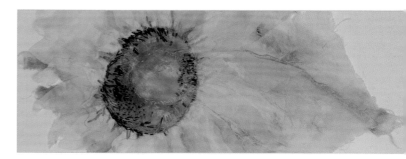

∧ *Daisy in Bloom* detail. The process for this piece is the same as *Poppy in Bloom,* using the daisy flower as inspiration.

< *Poppy in Bloom.* The image was painted loosely on cotton muslin (placed on newspaper) with acrylic paints. The muslin was dampened with water first so that the colours bled and allowed it to adhere to the paper. When dry, the muslin was folded, scrunched and torn. With some newspaper stuck to the back, it had an almost sculptural effect. Petals, cut from varying thicknesses of fabrics, were pinned around the centre, some pre-painted with acrylic paint, then stitched in place. French knots, seed and long/short stitches and beadwork were worked into the centre of the poppy.

∧ *Face of the Past* (from *Ancient Faces* series). Heavy machine embroidery on felt with additional metal shim added as a neckpiece. Inspiration came from an Egyptian grave painting.

< *Angel of Relocation.* Heavy machine embroidery on felt with the head-dress worked using the embellisher machine. Named by a friend who swore that this angel had master-minded Maggie and Clive's last house move.

Maggie Grey

Maggie has always loved drawing and painting. Her stitching career began when, in an attempt to enhance texture, she started adding random hand stitching to her watercolours and thought that she had invented mixed media. A City & Guilds exhibition soon put her right on that score and, having joined, she completed the course with a Distinction.

A meeting with the amazing Val Campbell-Harding and a shared love of, and fascination with, computer design led to team-teaching of the subject with Val in various colleges around the country. Further collaboration with Val led to them writing a book for the publisher B T Batsford, and Maggie went on to write many more books for this publisher.

There was such demand for courses on the 'new' idea of computer design and the use of digital design with sewing machines that Clive (with no regrets at all) abandoned his senior position in an insurance company to join her in teaching and together they ran many classes and summer schools all over the world. One of their proudest achievements was being part of a team developing textile modules for the Royal College of Art, Schools Technology Project. At this time, Maggie was also editor of *Embroidery* magazine for the Embroiderers' Guild.

Textiles have taken Maggie on a journey around the world, teaching by invitation in Australia, New Zealand, Canada where she had a most successful exhibition, and the USA.

Her exhibitions in the UK have included gallery shows with the exhibiting group Wessex Textiles and travelling exhibitions with the Knitting & Stitching Show. Her work is held in many private collections.

Her work is always inspiration-led, from the natural world to old manuscripts, from places to faces, especially old faces in grave paintings or statues – all is grist to the mill. Recent work has been concerned with story-telling and is generally mixed media, using paper as a base for hand stitching. She prefers to let inspiration lead the process rather than deciding on a technique first.

Growing out of a distance learning course, Workshop on the Web (WOW) was Maggie's next development. Her idea of a quarterly journal with step-by-step workshops by well-known tutors has led to the publication of this book, with its associated website. Publishing WOW as a book has only become possible because of her establishment of d4daisy books (*www.d4daisy.com*), a specialist publisher for textile art, in partnership with photographer Michael Wicks. D4daisy has published books by such noted textile artists as Valerie Campbell-Harding, Sue Rangeley, Jae Maries, Lynda Monk, the late Julia Caprara and, of course, Maggie herself.

Maggie is proud to be President of West Country Embroiderers, a group which takes in stitchers in the English counties of Cornwall, Dorset, Devon, Hampshire, Somerset and Wiltshire.

Her biggest ambition at the moment is to have more time to stitch as she has some great ideas just waiting to be unleashed.

Amanda House

Amanda has always enjoyed manipulating fabrics, stitching threads and using beads, as well as turning her hand to other crafts such as leaded glass, pastel painting and jewellery. Originally, she was taught traditional stitch work by her grandmother, but by 1998 had totally run out of enthusiasm. However, in 2008 she began to have a need to create again. In early 2009 she bought a new sewing machine and started to move more towards art quilts, one-off designs in jewellery and art dolls, embellishing, mixed media and found objects.

Often dyeing and manipulating her own fabrics and threads to achieve the effects she requires, Amanda's recent experiments have been concerned with ways of creating new fabrics from scratch, using scraps of old fabrics, threads and yarns. New products, or even old products used in a more innovative fashion, have been totally changing our view of textiles and she enjoys experimenting and making exciting new discoveries. Amanda loves hand stitch but also enjoys working on a domestic as well as a long arm sewing machine and her embellisher. She has found inspiration in the natural world and enjoys using organic shapes and forms, often in a more unusual style. Micro worlds and the suggestion of things that are hidden from view are hinted at in her work.

Amanda also produces innovative jewellery and beaded pieces, which sell out as soon as she can finish them.

She loves creating more sculptural pieces in the form of art dolls and mixed media compendiums, as well as numerous books in many styles in terms of both covers and content.

Having completed (and passed with Distinction) City & Guilds Creative Techniques – Textiles, as well as Levels 1 and 2 in Machine Embroidery, Amanda is a member of the Embroiderers' Guild, West Country Embroiderers, the Beadworkers' Guild and The Quilters' Guild of the British Isles. She has been published in *Workbox* magazine and *Workshop on the Web*. She was delighted to be on the front cover of a recent issue of *Dorset Artists* magazine.

Amanda exhibits widely in her own right, in addition to her joint exhibitions as a member of the Dorset Artists group. A great supporter of the Dorset arts scene, her lovely country home is always packed during Art Weeks. Her quilts, dolls and beaded pieces have won several awards.

A stalwart helper at Workshop on the Web, Amanda looks after the Members' Facebook page. In addition, she often writes articles for the publication, and her 2016 mixed media article 'Forest Floor' was an immediate hit which sparked much inspiration and resulting work on the Members' Facebook page. She demonstrated this technique to great effect at the subsequent Craft 4 Crafters show.

> *Relic: Jurassic.* This piece was built using many layers. It started with a hand-dyed cloth which was over-printed with a large ammonite stencil. Space-dyed threads and yarns were used for the stitching which added texture and movement. The small panels continue the theme of the ammonites, with the printed text telling the story of their era and how they became part of the fabric of our land.

Angie Hughes

Angie Hughes is an artist and tutor who lives and works in Ledbury in the beautiful English county of Herefordshire. She has been interested in textiles since she left school although only discovered creative embroidery in 1994 when she began studying City & Guilds at Malvern Hills College. This course taught her to experiment with different materials and techniques and she has continued to begin new projects in this 'hands on' manner ever since.

While a student, she won the prestigious Charles Henry Foyle Trust Award for Stitched Textiles with her piece 'Unfolding Word', and her work entitled 'Shroud' was accepted for the Embroiderers' Guild's popular Art of the Stitch exhibition. She carried on her studies at Gloucestershire College of Arts and Technology (GLOSCAT) with Liz Harding, after which she discovered a talent for teaching. She has spent time honing her skills on the sewing machine and all her pieces make use of machine embroidery at some stage of their construction.

Angie's work is influenced by many themes but poetry or text play a big part. She also finds inspiration in the natural world, with a particular interest in plant forms. A friend describes her as a process-based artist and she would agree, always enjoying placing a pile of paints, printing blocks and fabrics on her work table, pondering ways of making something new and exciting. This kind of jigsaw process is reflected in her current work.

Angie has recently enjoyed developing work that focuses on gardens that were once tamed but attempt – and often succeed – in becoming wild. She enjoys the juxtaposition of randomly 'placed' plants alongside the order the gardener tries to contain. Imagining these gardens in shadowy moonlit illumination, her colours have become almost monochromatic, silvers and blacks and those hard-to-name colours that are revealed when light has faded. From drawings and photographs, Angie has developed her visual ideas through embroidery, inventing simplified botanical forms. This recent work has seen her explore discharged and painted velvets, heat-transferred foils and layered organza, all of which are intensely machine embroidered.

She teaches to guilds and groups all over the British Isles and has also taught in Australia and New Zealand. Her book *Stitch, Cloth, Paper & Paint* is a bestseller for Search Press. Angie has also featured in many publications including *Embroidery; Stitch* magazine; *Workshop on the Web; Cloth, Paper, Scissors; Quilting Arts; Hot Textiles* by Kim Thittichai; and *The Encyclopaedia of Embroidery* by Val Holmes.

∧ *Six Flowers.* This is one of a continuous collection of pieces by Angie, inspired by gardens at twilight. They are made from cotton velvet which has been printed, collaged and stitched.

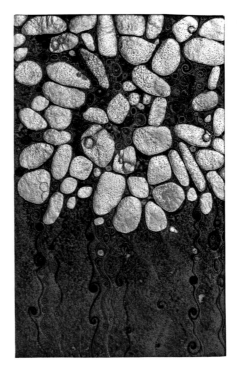

< *From the Shore to the Sea.* An observation piece constructed after watching the water, when the tide goes out, running in rivulets through stones on the shore, then through the sand and into the sea.

Samantha Packer

Sam Packer came from a background of theatre, film and media although, having a mother who embroiders, stitch was always on the periphery. When children arrived on the scene, a change of pace and focus led her to textiles once again and, from 2006, she contributed regularly to Workshop on the Web, reviewing products, books and exhibitions as well as interviewing celebrities.

The past couple of years has seen her reach a crossroads as her children are older and this has allowed her once more to devote time to making and stitching. Anyone who has seen Sam's workspace knows she is a messy worker and so she has used this time to embark on a radical de-clutter. She would recommend it to anyone wanting to clear their head and work out how they want their work to progress. A combination of this, and the purchase of a roll of teabag paper that turned out to be the size of small car, has given her a more limited materials list but a clearer idea of what she wants to make.

Sam's areas of interest are paper, cloth, words and letters, machine embroidery and mixed media. She has recently started teaching workshops, mainly in mixed media techniques that can be translated to textiles. Anyone who has seen her demonstrations on the Workshop on the Web stand at Craft 4 Crafters will know that she is a whizz on the gelli-plate and has some great ideas for stencils.

Having co-authored the d4daisy book *Cut, Shape, Stitch*, her favourite piece was a mixed media feather cape and it has led to the development of a series of capes – currently work in progress. These will be showcased in 2018 when Sam gives her first talk. At least one will be made of teabag paper.

Sam has a website, ***www.samanthapacker.com*** which is frequently updated with book and exhibition reviews and she is regularly found on social media (Instagram is the best place to find her). She has loved the opportunity to interview Jan Beaney and Jean Littlejohn for this book as it allowed her to read through their whole back catalogue of books in one sitting.

∧ This stitched collar was designed and cut on the Brother Scan'N'Cut machine using leaf motifs. Free machine embroidery was then worked on hand-dyed fabric and Vlieseline Style-Vil. Hand embroidery and beads were added using threads from Mulberry Silks.

Distant Stitch

Inspirational Online Textile and Design Courses

www.distantstitch.co.uk

- Embroidery
- Machine Embroidery
- Creative Sketchbooks
- Patchwork & Quilting

email Siân Martin

sian@distantstitch.co.uk
www.distantstitch.co.uk

Try our FREE Taster...make a beautiful bag in hand or machine stitching

artVanGo the studios

Creating with Colour! since 1989

Everything for mixed-media and creative textile art!!
Shop·Mail Order·Online Shop·Exhibitions·Workshops!

www.artvango.co.uk   Tel: 01438 814946

MULBERRY SILKS

Patricia Wood supplies by mail order, hand wound packs of pure thread in beautiful colour schemes. Mini Topics/Silk Topics/Connoisseur Range and Palettes. Silk Fabrics – Silk Ribbons – Double-sided Velvet ribbons and more — for the discerning embroiderer

mulberrysilks@btinternet.com
www.mulberrysilks-patriciawood.com

Sonas Studio

Kim Thittichai's *Experimental Textiles* courses can now be done online!

On the Surface, Newspaper Faux Chenille, Manipulating with Heat, Scrumptious Spunbond and more

Courses consists of videos, tips & techniques. They are process based, with encouragement to find your own way with a technique

info@kimthittichai.com   www.sonas-studio.com

35a St Andrews Road, Portslade, East Sussex. BN41 1DB

GILLSEW
Embroidery Supplies

Whether you are a beginner or an expert, you still need supplies. We stock many of the products a good textile student needs

Including hand and machine threads, soluble fabrics, transfer foils, kunin felt, modelling fabrics, inkjet printer fabric, heat transfer paper, Indian printing blocks and a great deal more

**Visit us at www.gillsew.co.uk
or phone 01494 881886 for more information**

double trouble
enterprises

  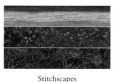

Stitchscapes

Double Trouble Enterprises publishes books and DVDs to promote further interest in embroidery and allied subjects. We are Jan Beaney and Jean Littlejohn, internationally known textiles artists, authors and tutors. Our aim is to give students the confidence to design and create their own unique work

www.doubletrouble-ent.com   sales@doubletrouble-ent.com